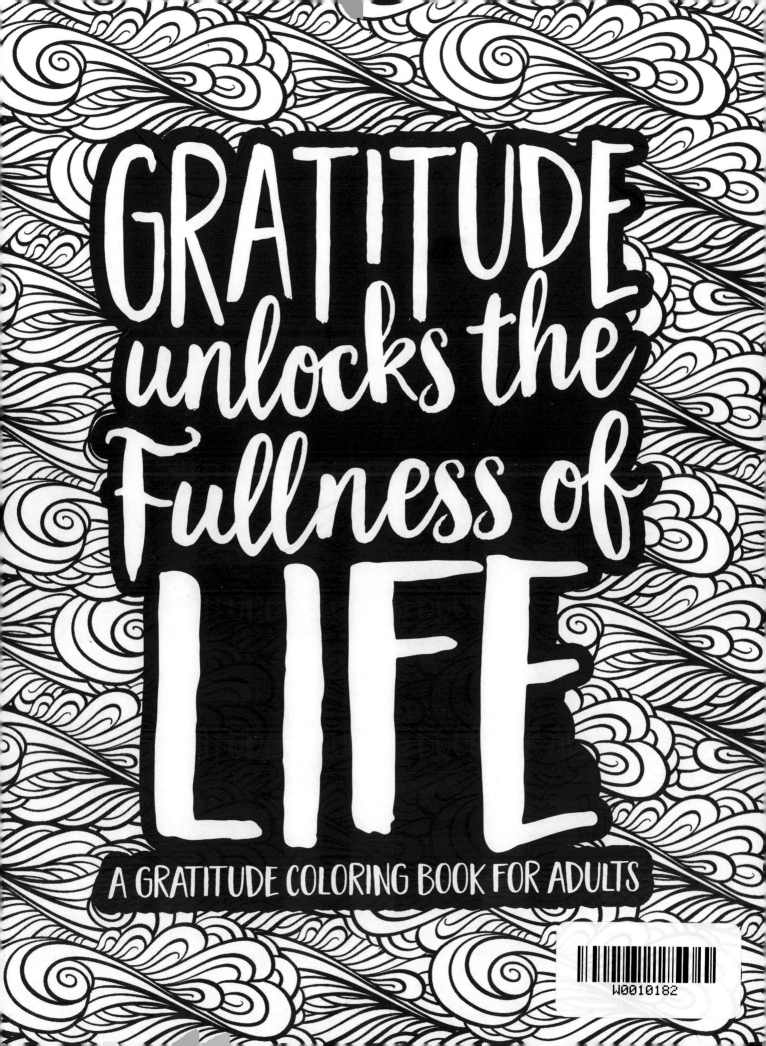

GRATITUDE unlocks the Fullness of LIFE

A GRATITUDE COLORING BOOK FOR ADULTS

Want free goodies?
Email us at freebies@pbleu.com

@papeteriebleu

Papeterie Bleu

Shop our other books at
www.pbleu.com

Wholesale distribution through Ingram Content Group
www.ingramcontent.com/publishers/distribution/wholesale

For questions and customer service, email us at
support@pbleu.com

ISBN: 9781640017412

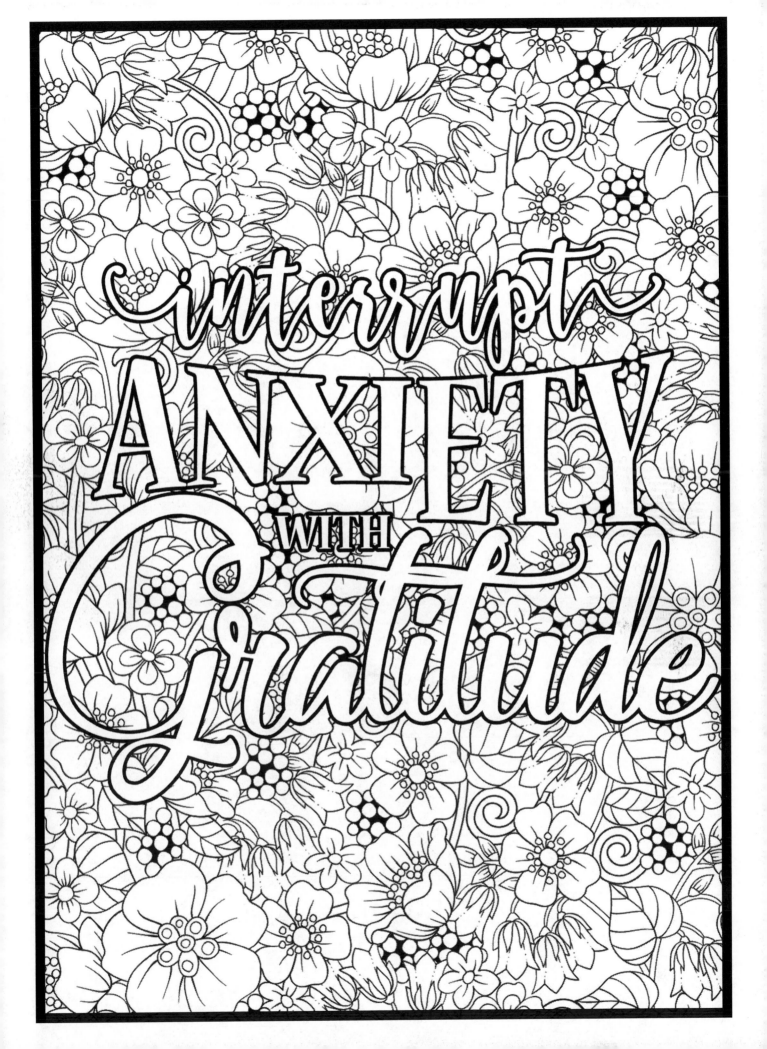

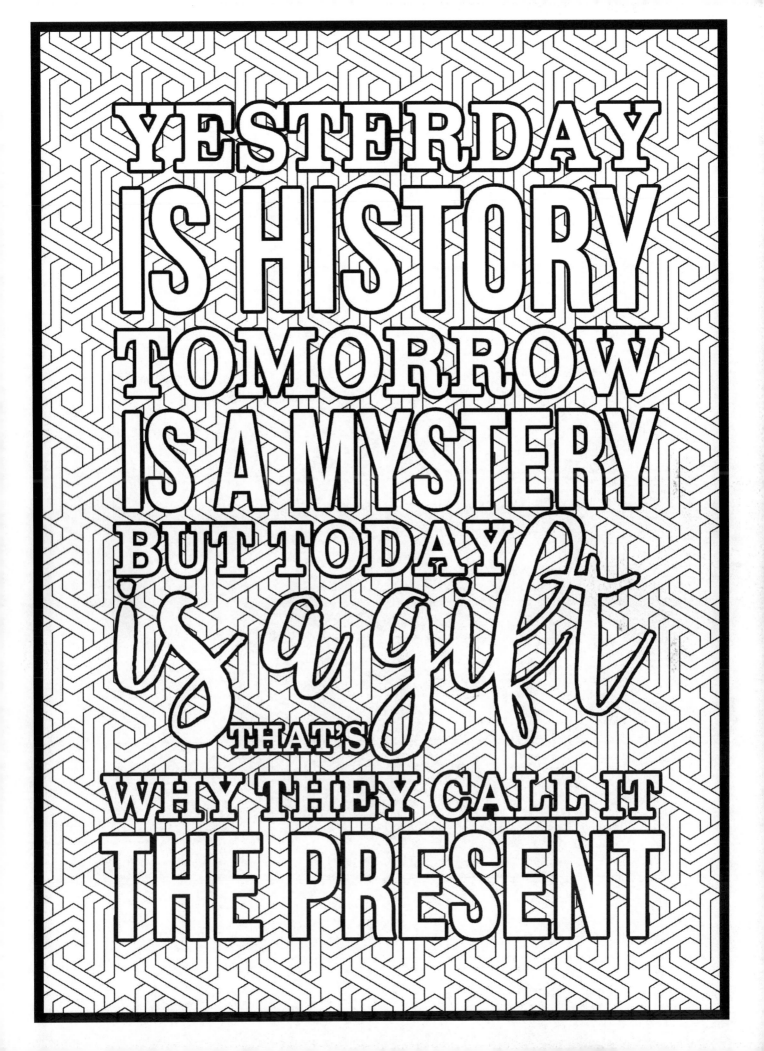

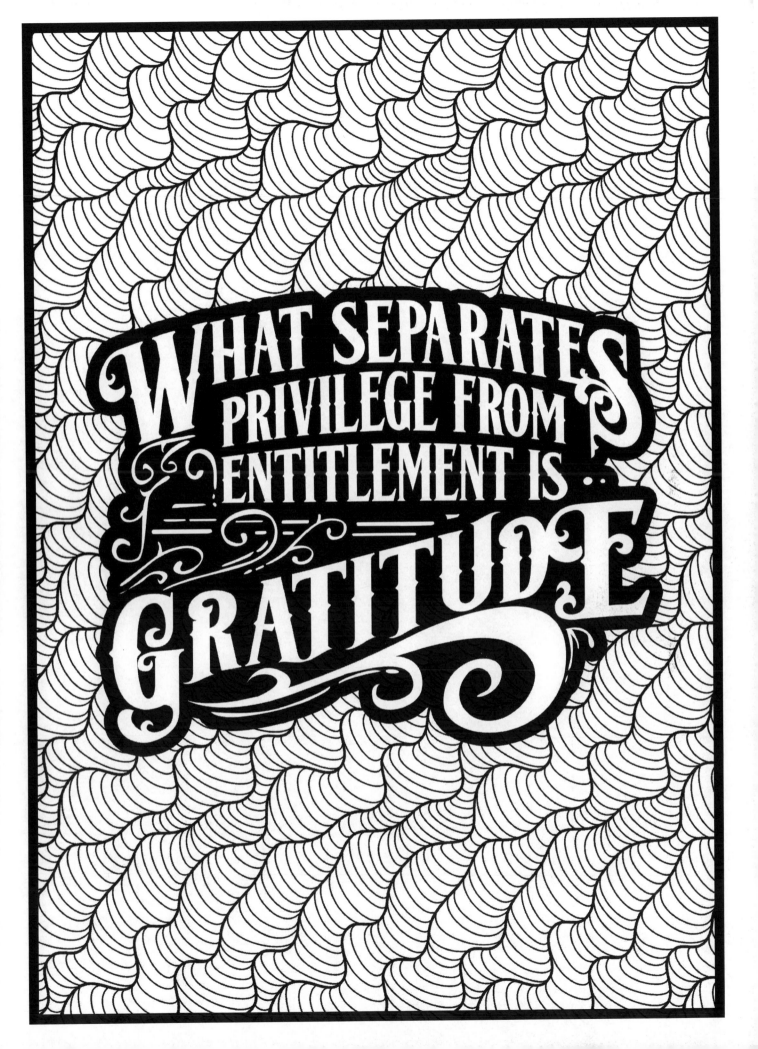

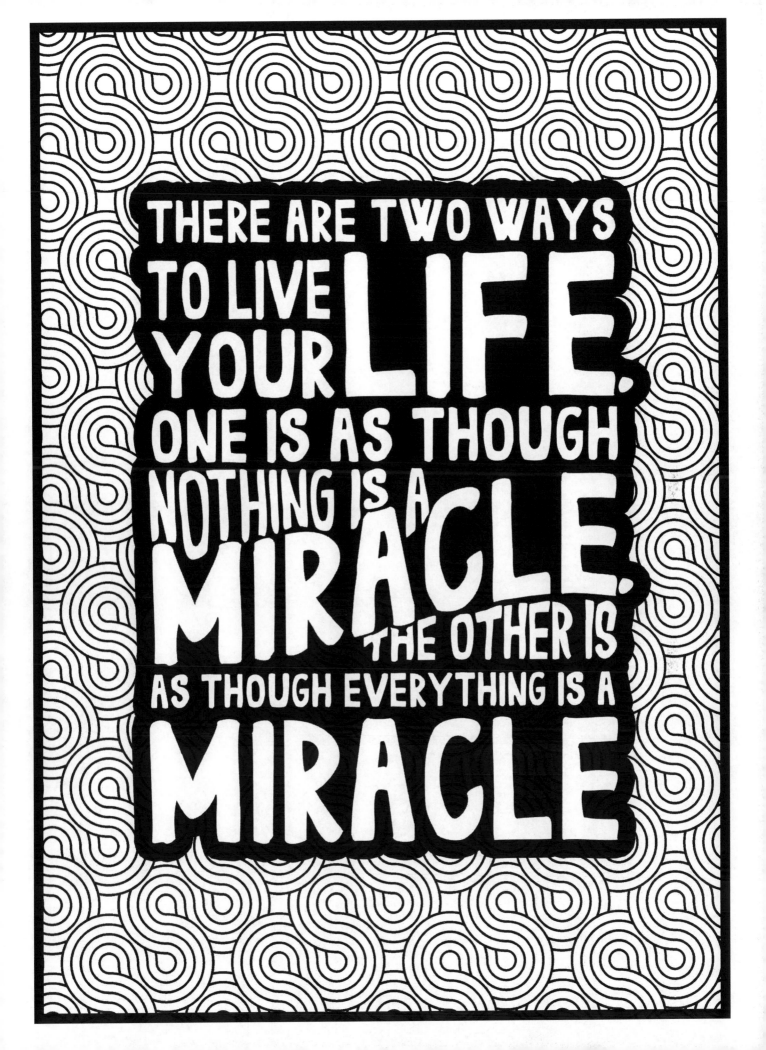

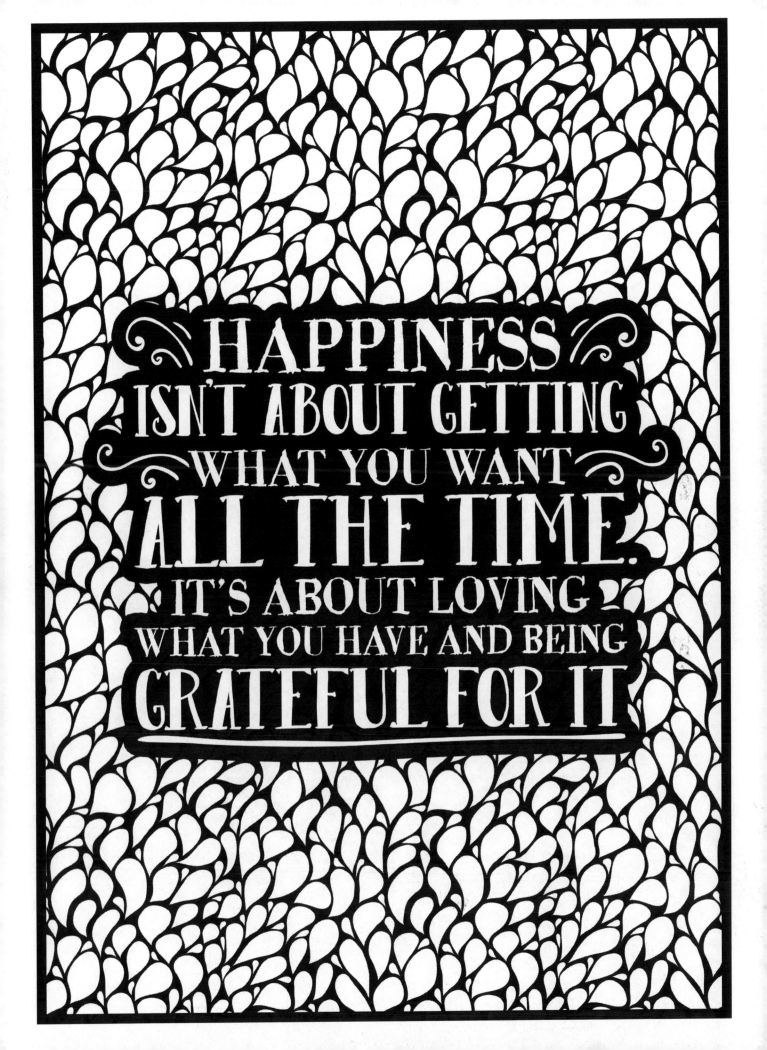

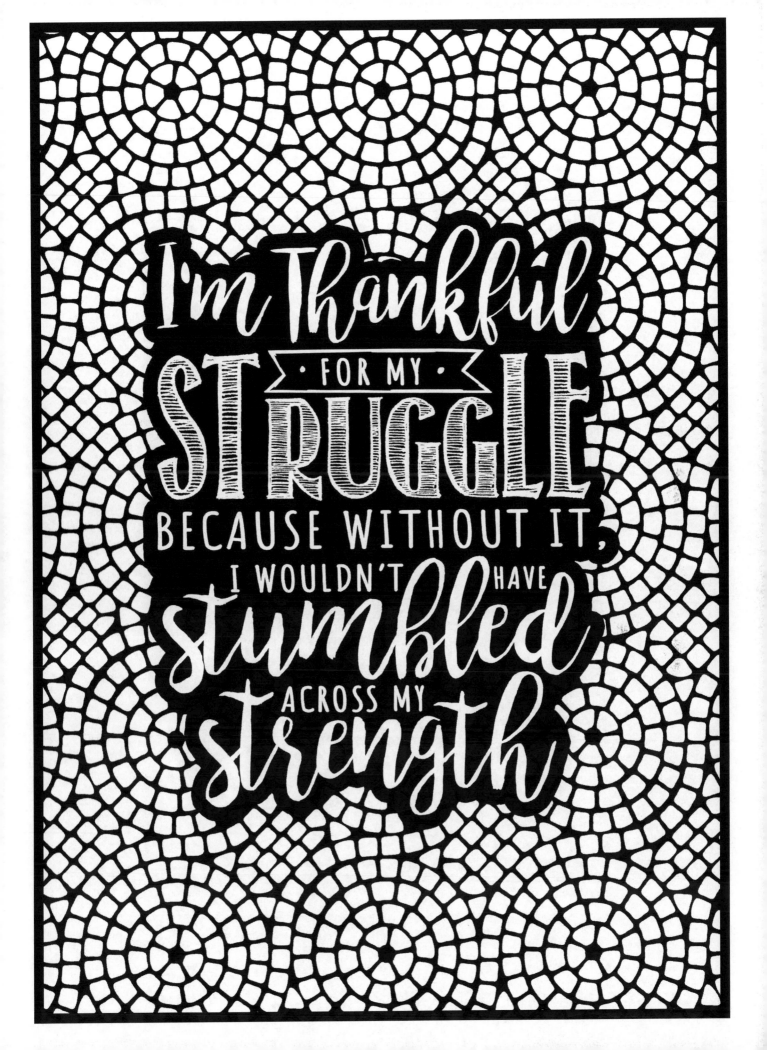

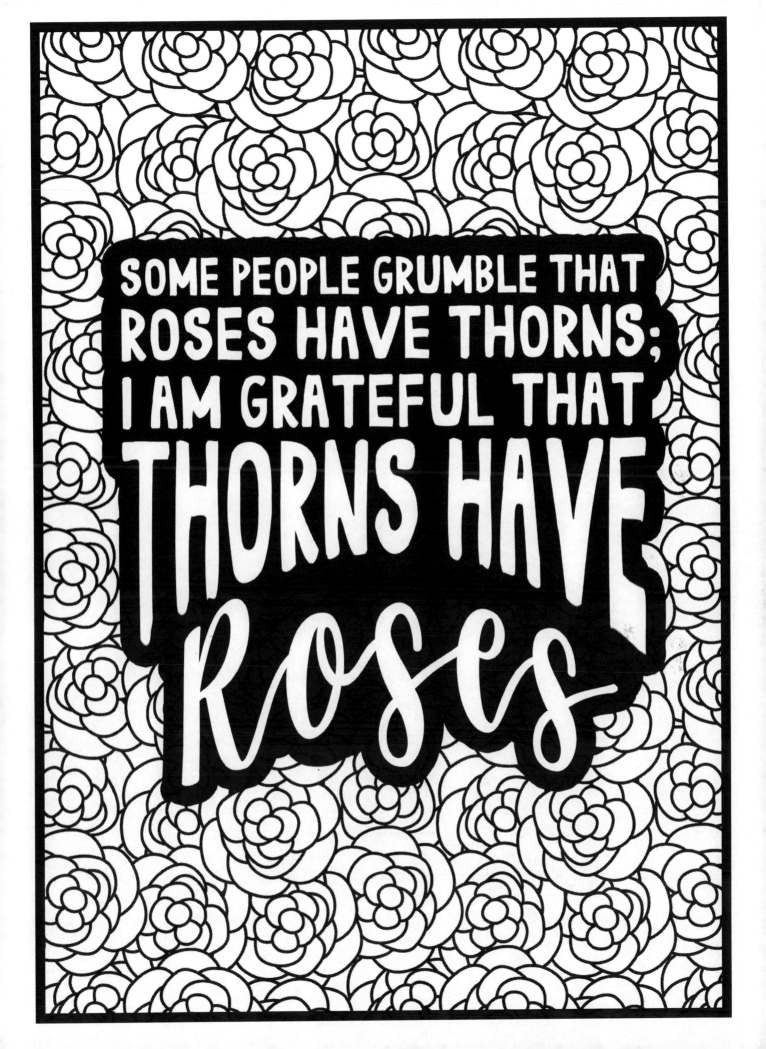

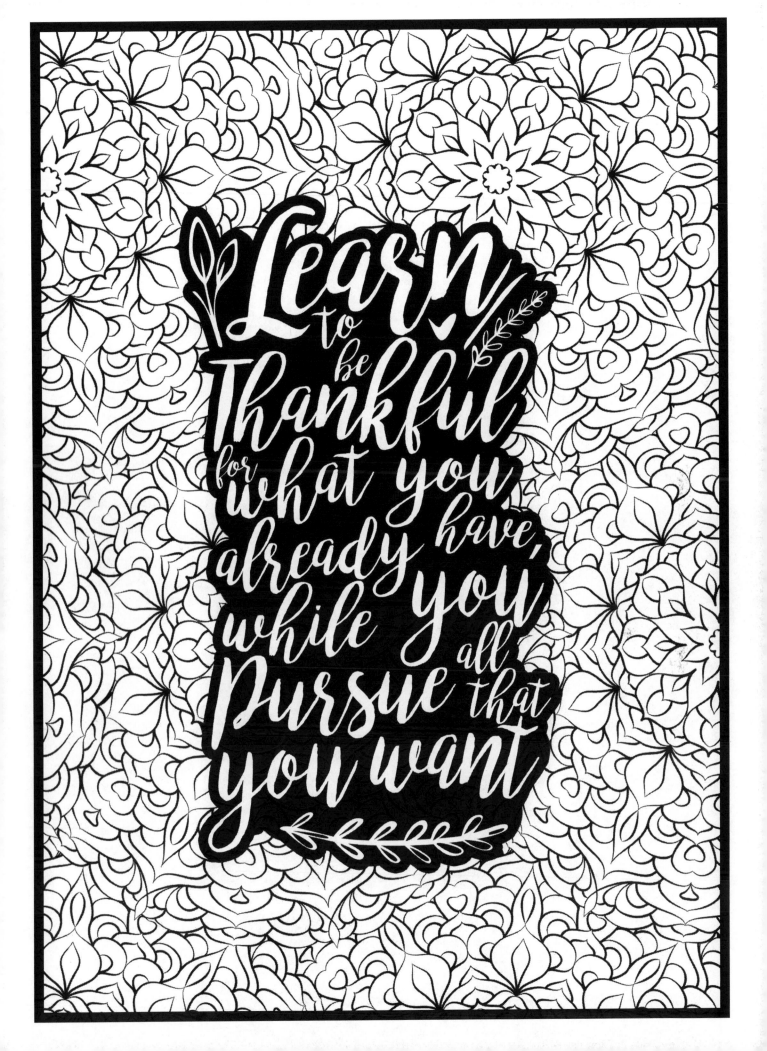

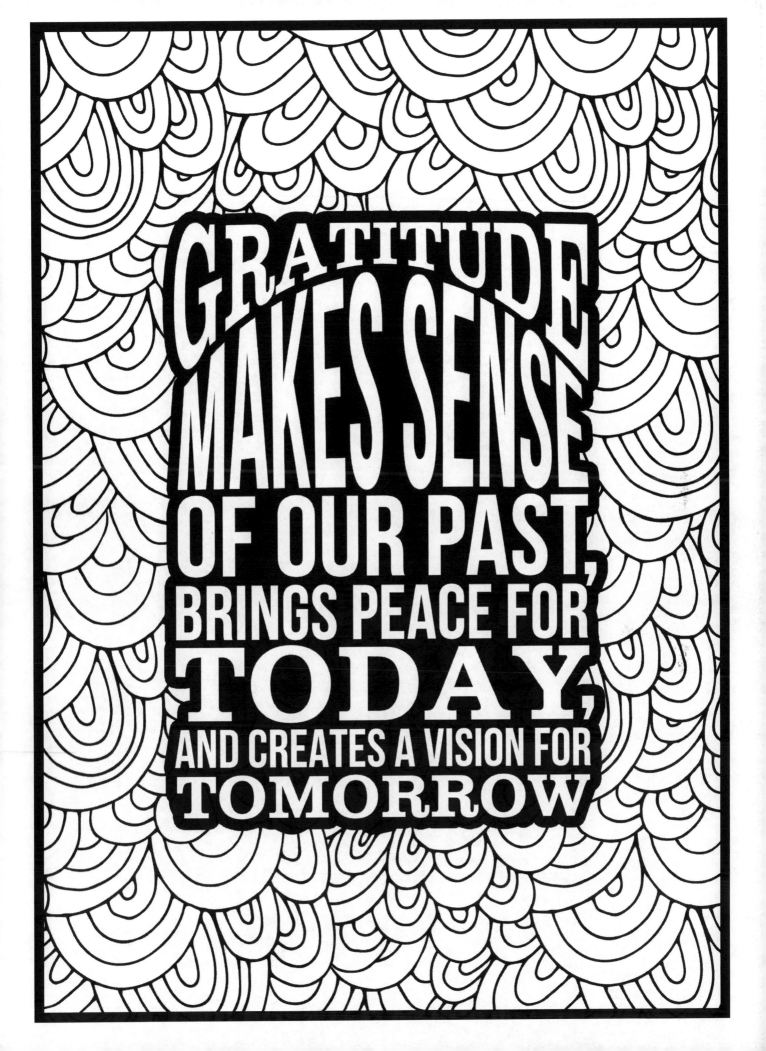

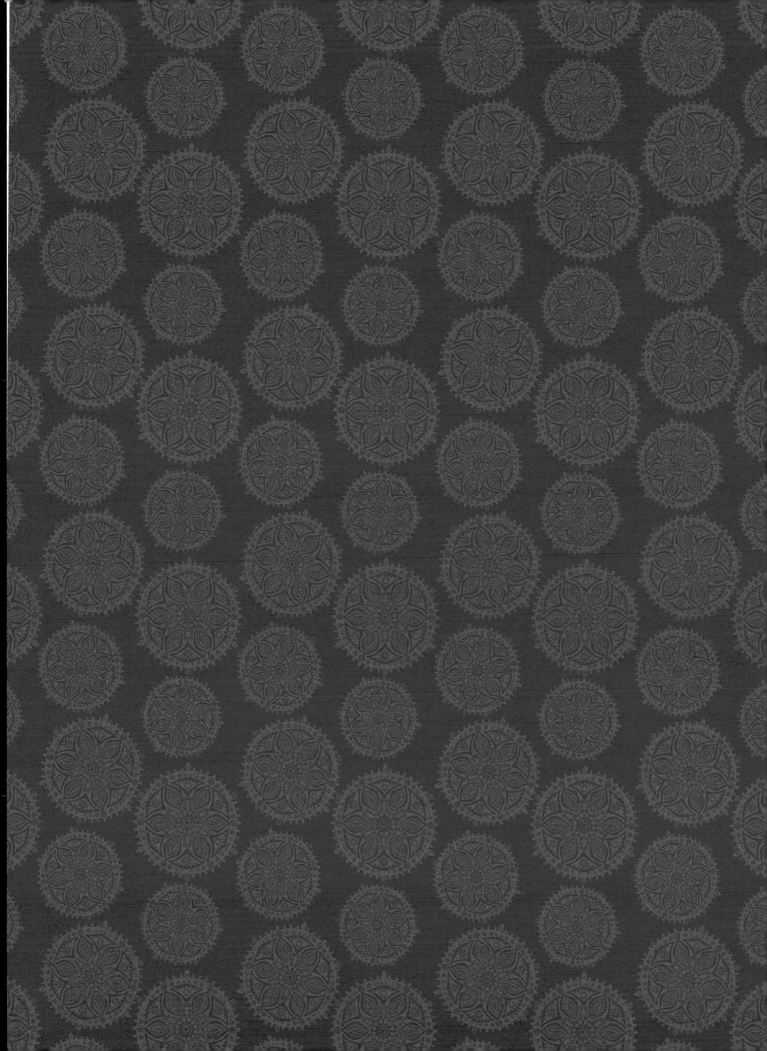

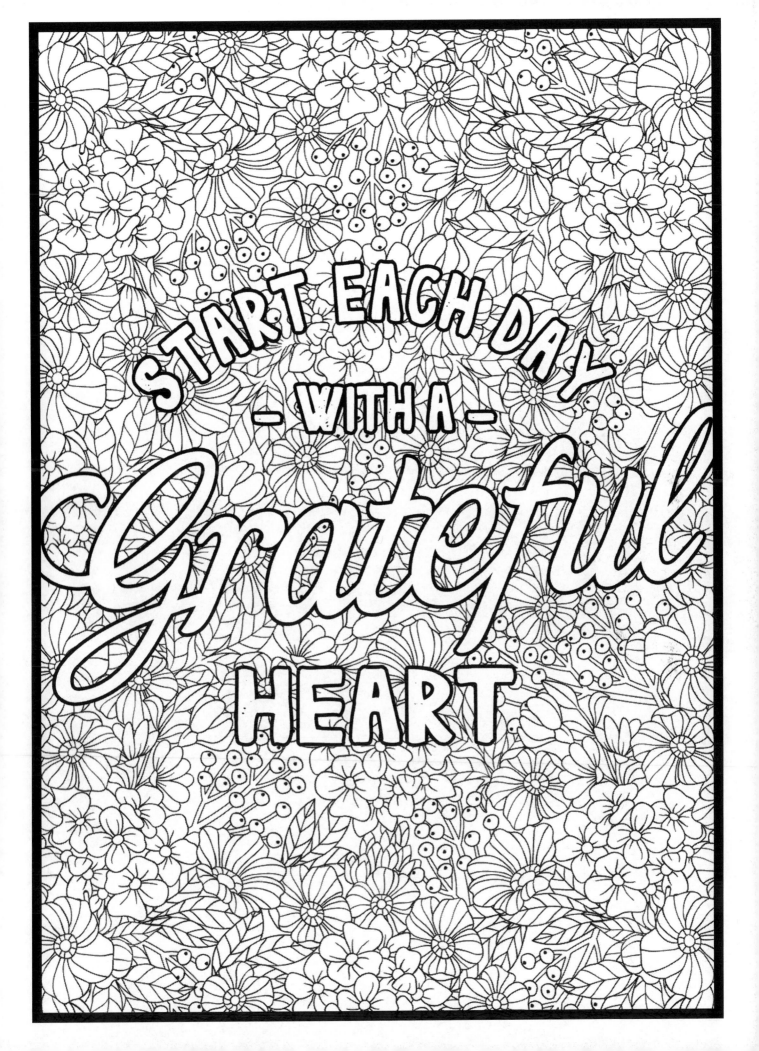

STOP. NOW enjoy THE moment. it's now OR NEVER

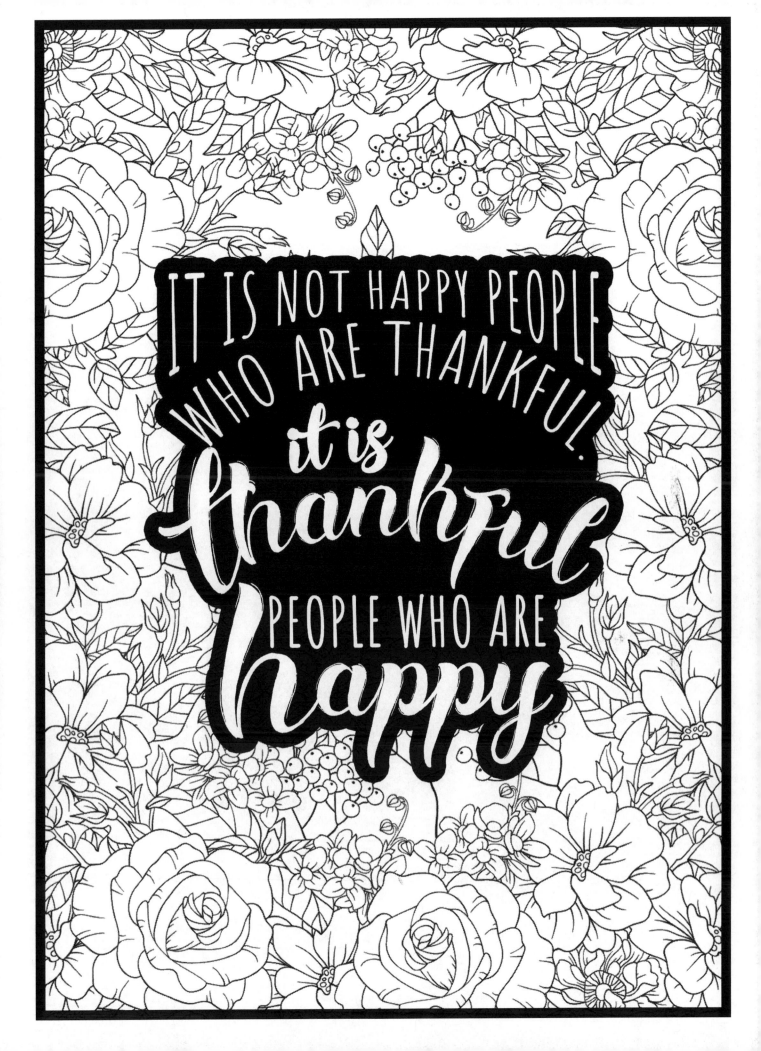

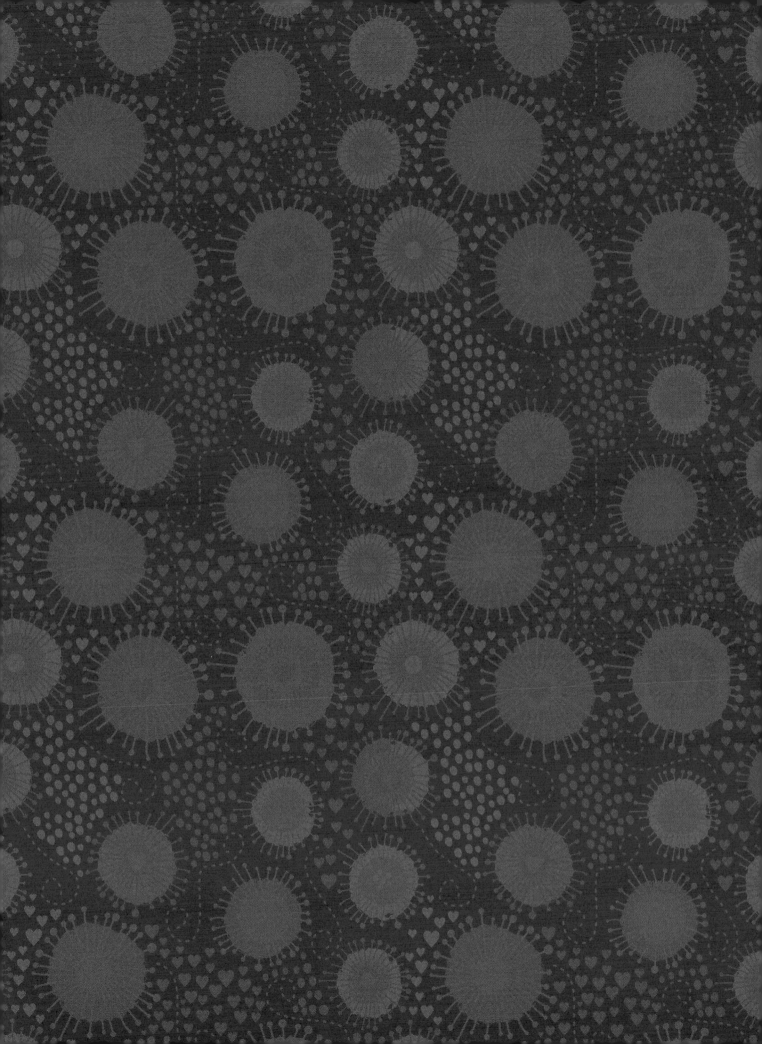

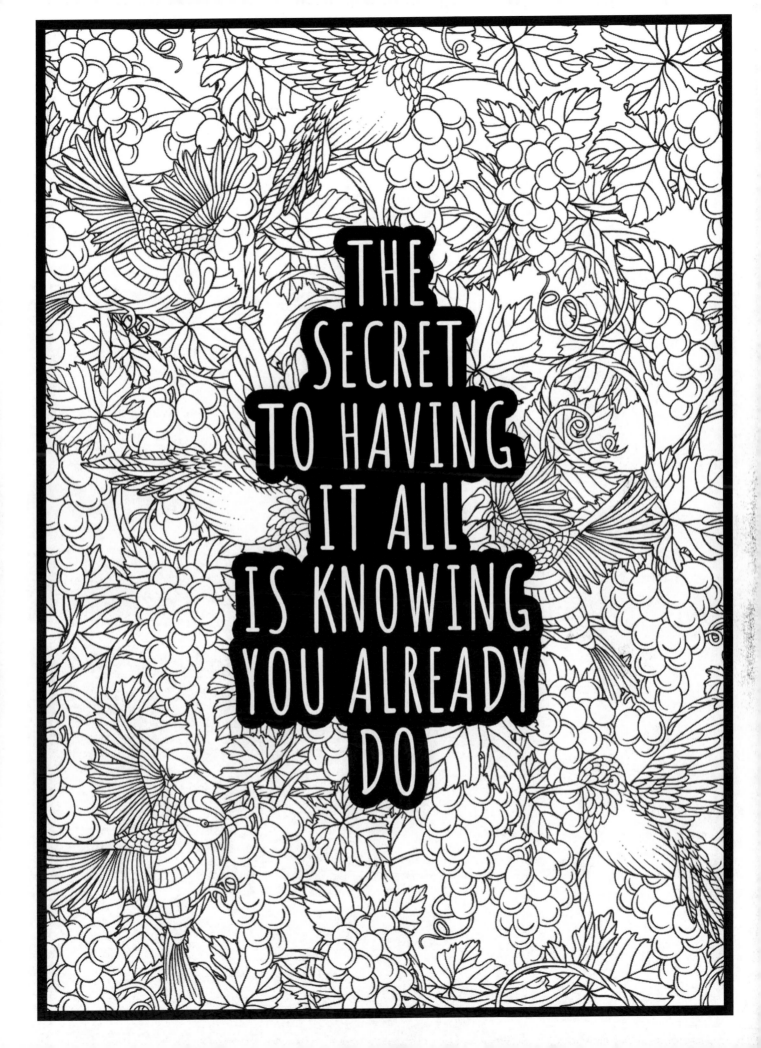

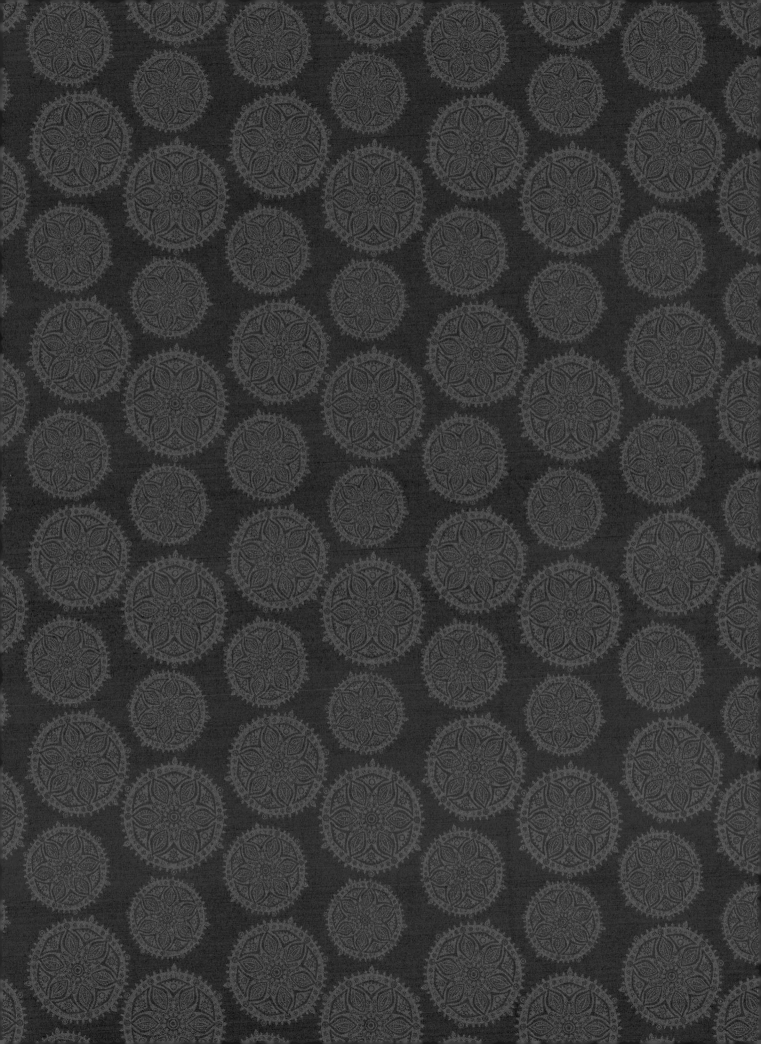

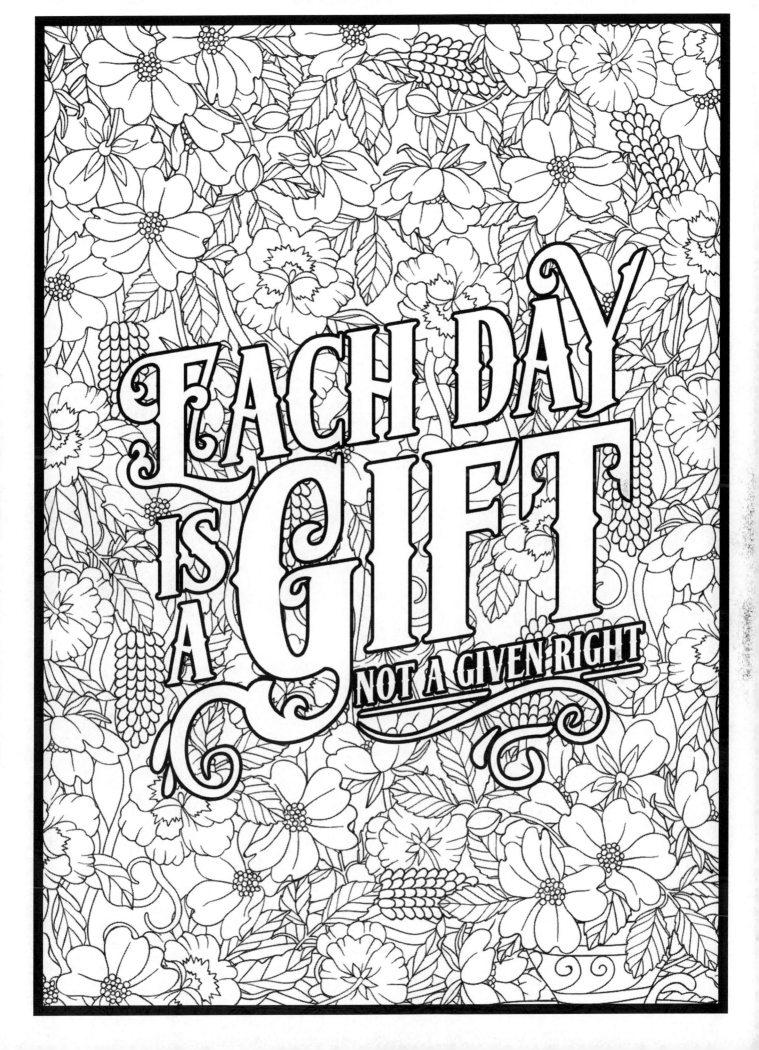

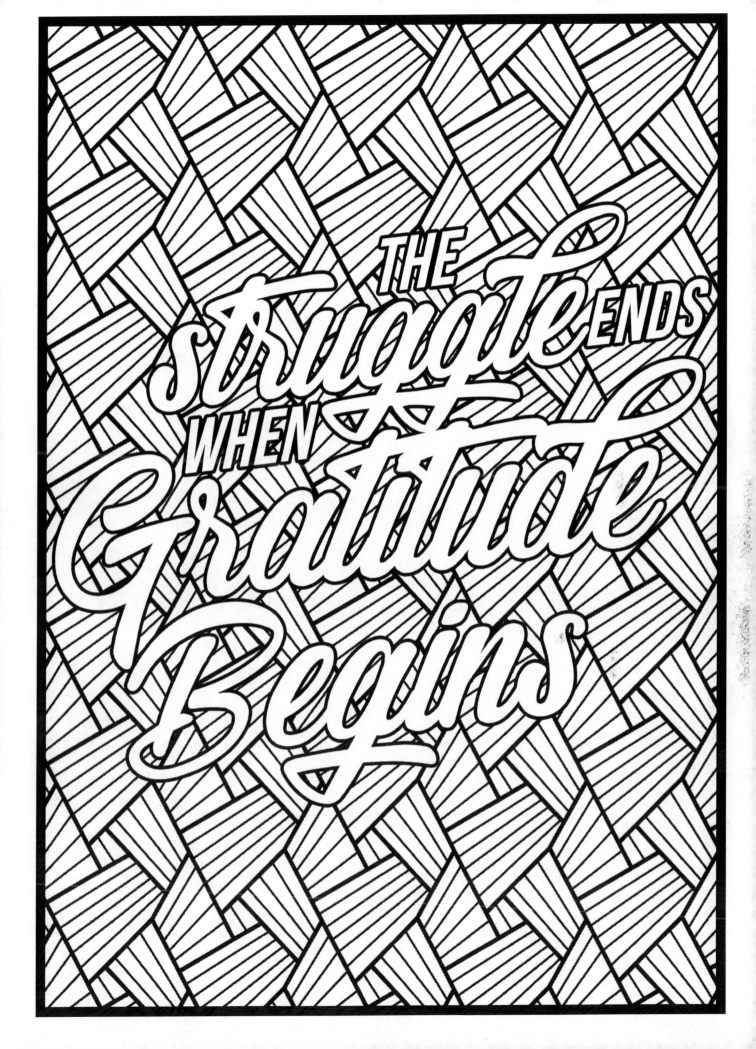

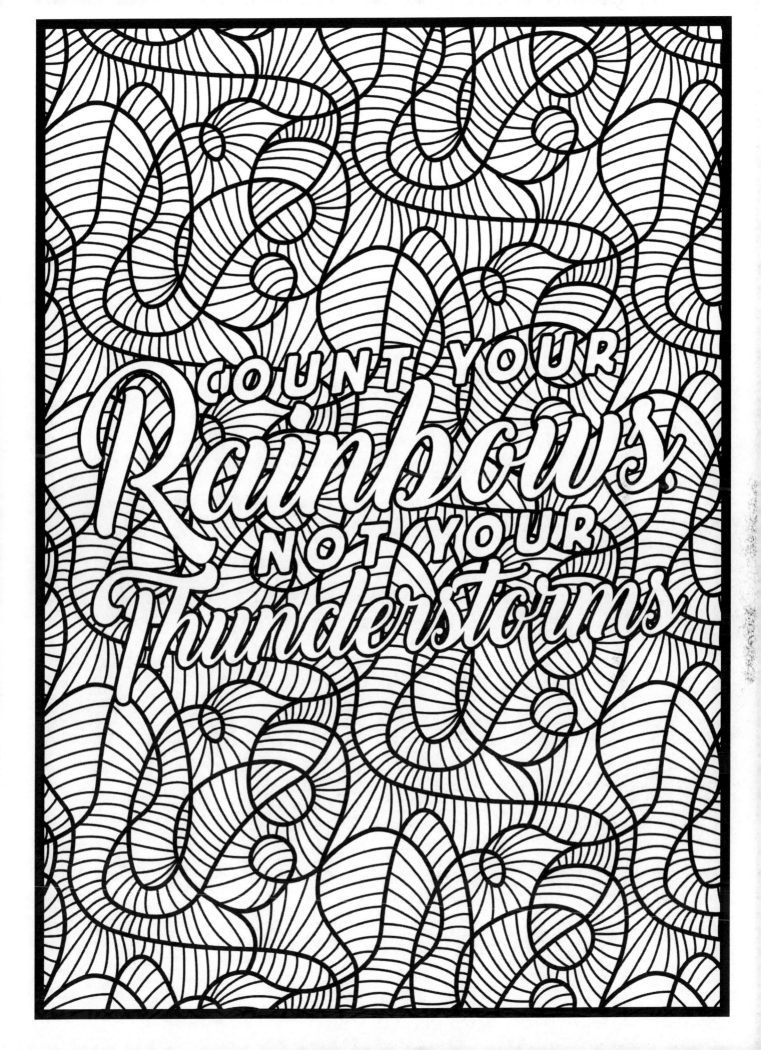

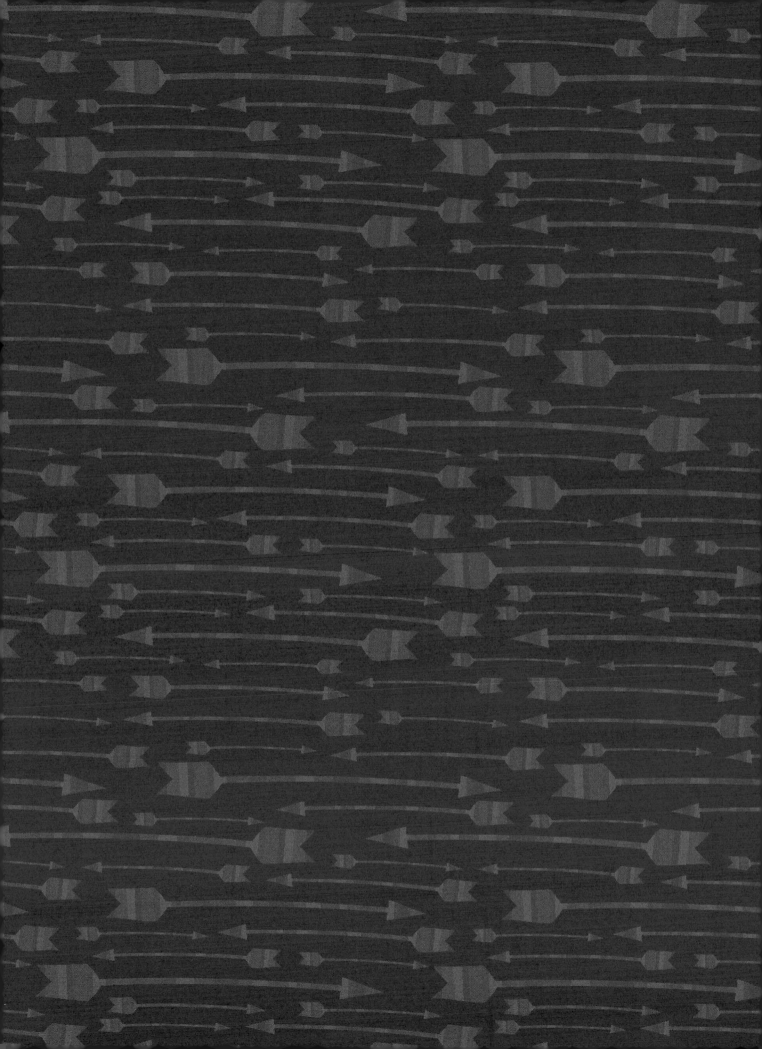

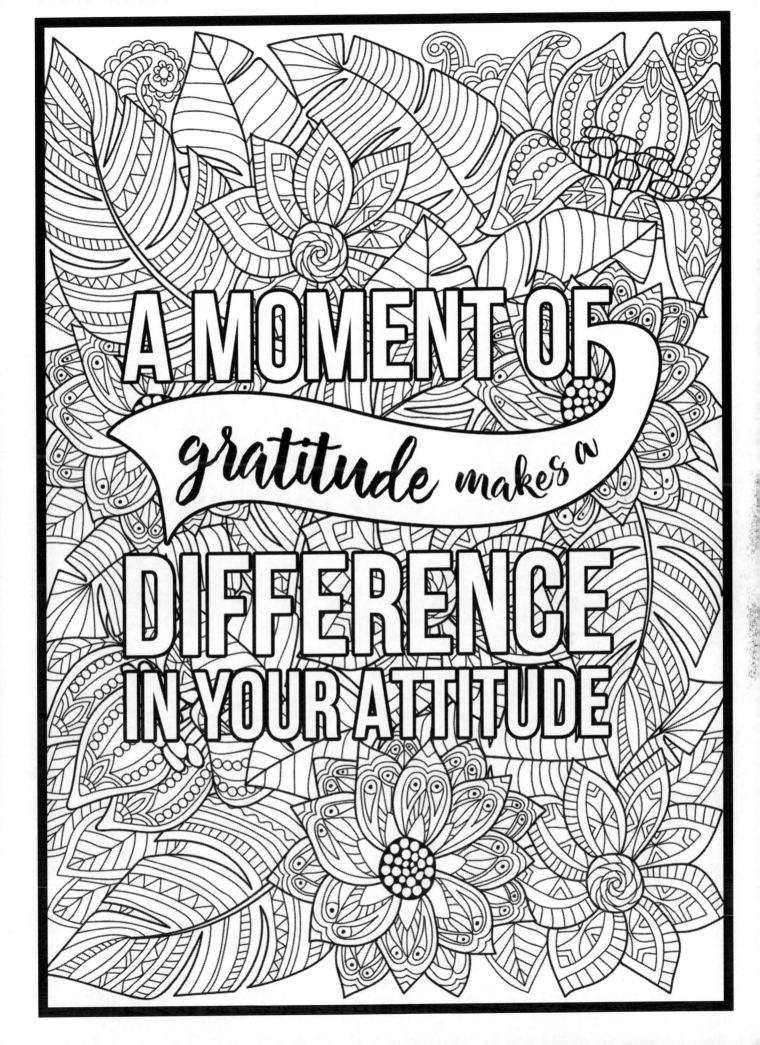

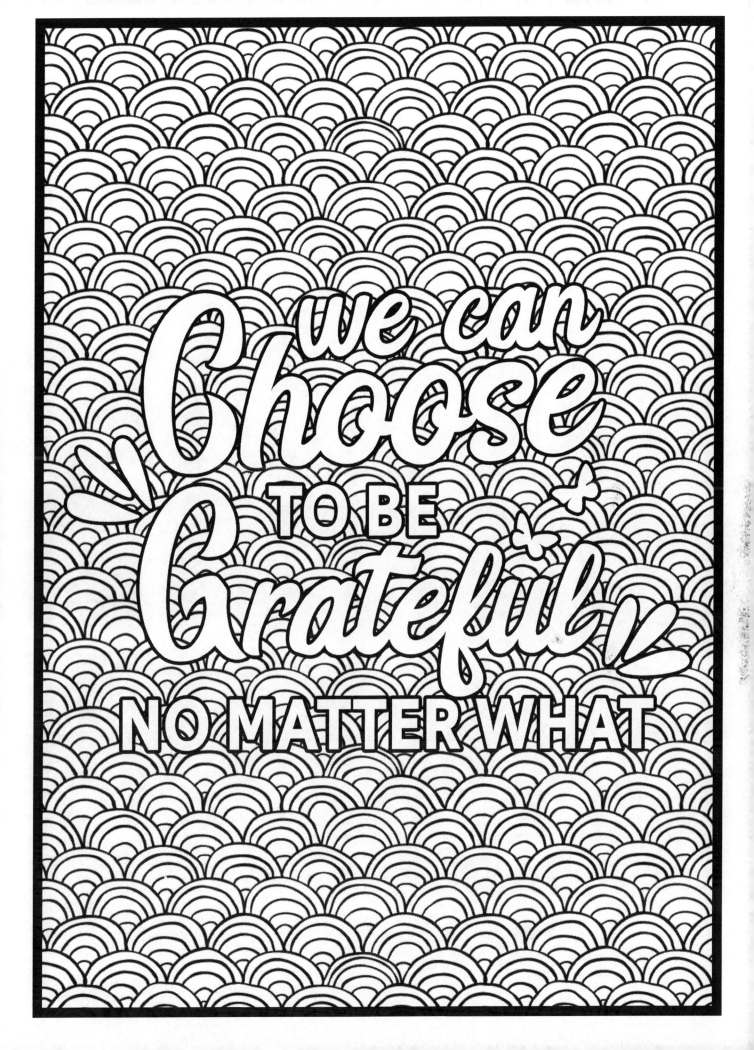

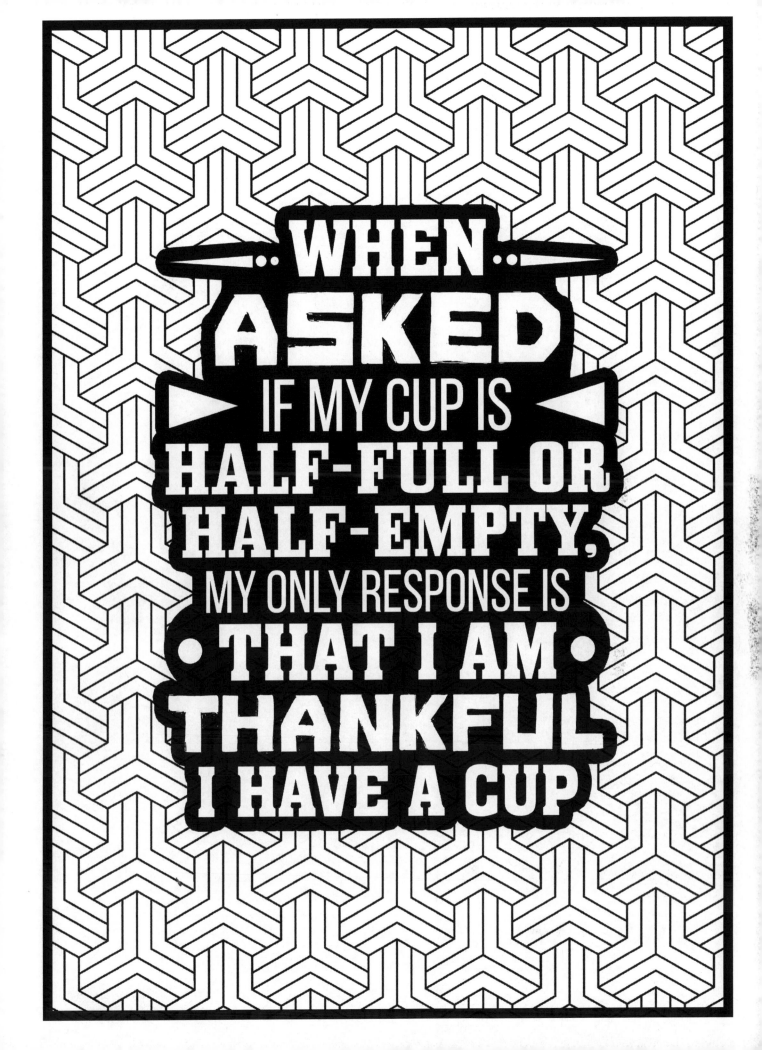

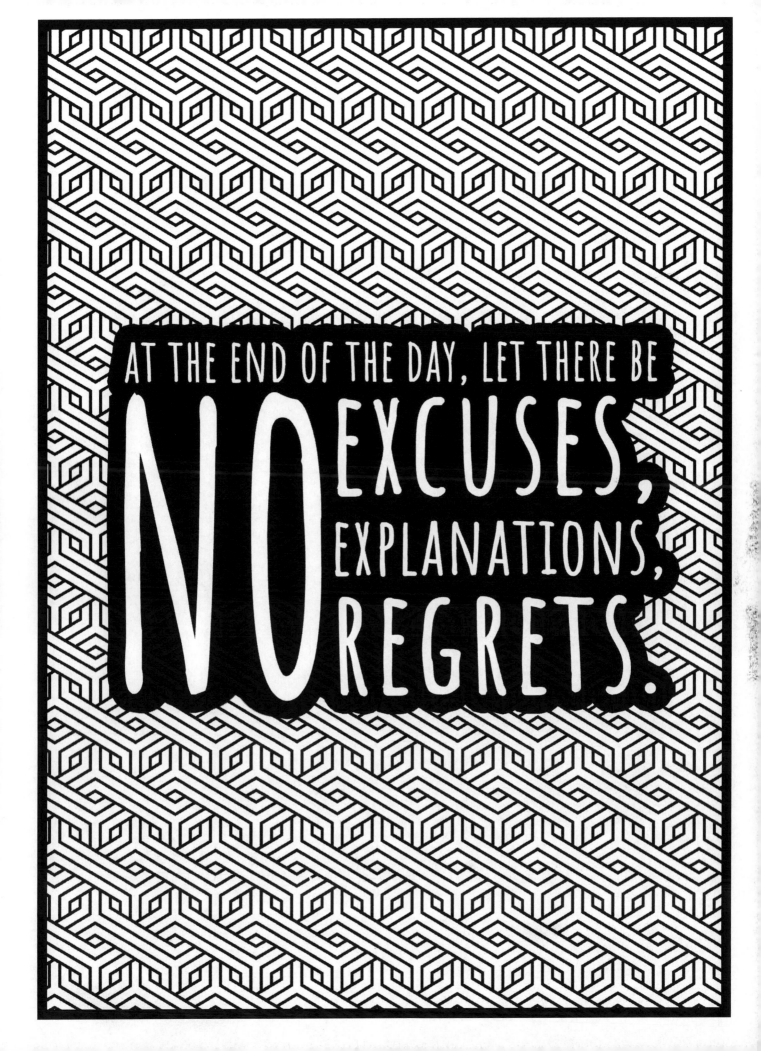

FREE PDF DOWNLOAD OF THIS BOOK

www.pbleu.com/grateful

YOUR DOWNLOAD CODE: GRT3673

@papeteriebleu

Papeterie Bleu

Want free goodies?
Email us at freebies@pbleu.com

@papeteriebleu

Papeterie Bleu

Shop our other books at
www.pbleu.com

Wholesale distribution through Ingram Content Group
www.ingramcontent.com/publishers/distribution/wholesale

For questions and customer service, email us at
support@pbleu.com

Made in the USA
Coppell, TX
13 November 2020